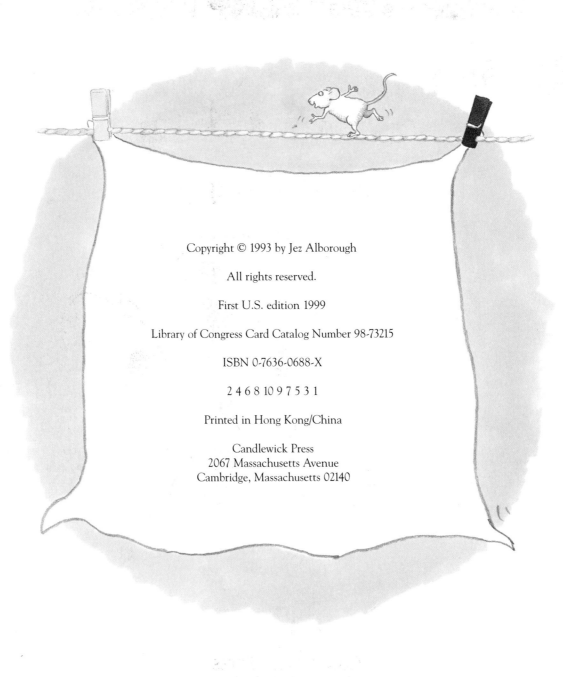

First U.S. edition 1999

Library of Congress Card Catalog Number 98-73215

ISBN 0-7636-0688-X

2 4 6 8 10 9 7 5 3 1

Printed in Hong Kong/China

Candlewick Press
2067 Massachusetts Avenue
Cambridge, Massachusetts 02140

A FLIP-THE-FLAP BOOK
Whose Socks Are Those?

Jez Alborough

CANDLEWICK PRESS
CAMBRIDGE, MASSACHUSETTS

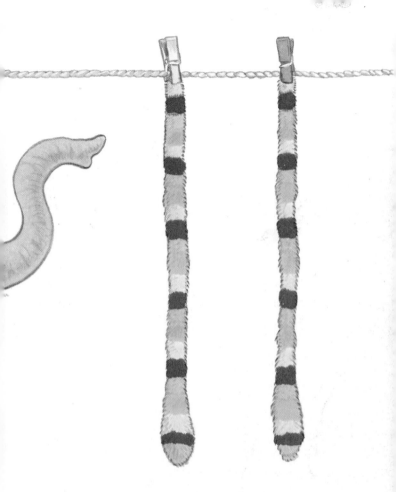

asked the elephant.

asked the elephant
and the flamingo.

grunted the
orangutan.

asked the elephant,
the flamingo,
and the orangutan.

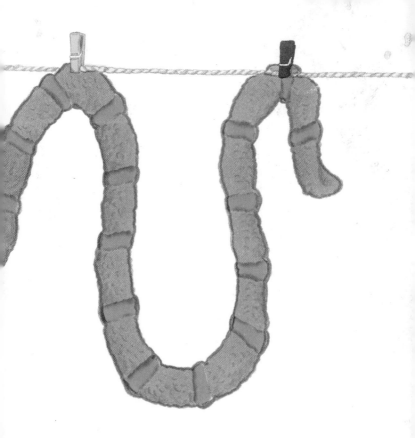

asked the elephant,
the flamingo,
the orangutan,
and the mouse.

asked the flamingo,
the orangutan,
the mouse,
and the giraffe.

What are we going to do now tha we're all wearing our dry clothes?

asked the flamingo,
the orangutan,
the mouse,
and the giraffe.

MAY   2000